LEADERS IN MY COMMUNITY

I WANT TO BE MAYOR

by Jennifer Boothroyd

Consultant: Beth Gambro
Reading Specialist, Yorkville, Illinois

BEARPORT
PUBLISHING

Minneapolis, Minnesota

Teaching Tips

Before Reading
- Look at the cover of the book. Discuss the picture and the title.
- Ask readers to brainstorm a list of what they already know about mayors. What can they expect to see in the book?
- Go on a picture walk, looking through the pictures to discuss vocabulary and make predictions about the text.

During Reading
- Read for purpose. Encourage readers to think about the city they live in as they are reading.
- Ask readers to look for the details of the book. What are they learning about the job of a mayor?
- If readers encounter an unknown word, ask them to look at the sounds in the word. Then, ask them to look at the rest of the page. Are there any clues to help them understand?

After Reading
- Encourage readers to pick a buddy and reread the book together.
- Ask readers to name two things a mayor does. Find the pages that tell about these things.
- Ask readers to write or draw something they learned about being mayor.

Credits:
Cover and title page, © jaroon/iStock and © refrina/Shutterstock; 3, © EugeneF/Adobe Stock; 5, © Brocreative/Adobe Stock; 6–7, © fstop123/iStock; 9, © Monkey Business Images/Shutterstock; 10–11, © dbvirago/Adobe Stock; 13, © Frances Roberts/Alamy; 14–15, © ZUMA Press Inc / Alamy Stock Photo/Alamy; 17, © Ridofranz/iStock; 18–19, © Sheila Fitzgerald/Shutterstock; 21, © FatCamera/iStock; 22T, © Goodboy Picture Company/iStock; 22M, © FreeProd/Adobe Stock; 22B, © RgStudio/iStock; 23TL, © DanielJohn/Shutterstock; 23TM, © BearFotos/Shutterstock; 23TR, © Flamingo Images/Adobe Stock; 23BL, © FatCamera/iStock; 23BR, © rawpixel.com/Adobe Stock.

STATEMENT ON USAGE OF GENERATIVE ARTIFICIAL INTELLIGENCE
Bearport Publishing remains committed to publishing high-quality nonfiction books. Therefore, we restrict the use of generative AI to ensure accuracy of all text and visual components pertaining to a book's subject. See BearportPublishing.com for details.

Library of Congress Cataloging-in-Publication Data

Names: Boothroyd, Jennifer, 1972- author.
Title: I want to be mayor / by Jennifer Boothroyd.
Description: Minneapolis, Minnesota : Bearport Publishing Company, 2024. |
  Series: Leaders in my community | Includes bibliographical references
  and index.
Identifiers: LCCN 2023028228 (print) | LCCN 2023028229 (ebook) | ISBN
  9798889162674 (library binding) | ISBN 9798889162728 (paperback) | ISBN
  9798889162766 (ebook)
Subjects: LCSH: Mayors--United States--Juvenile literature. | Municipal
  government--United States--Juvenile literature.
Classification: LCC JS356 .B66 2024 (print) | LCC JS356 (ebook) | DDC
  352.23/2160973--dc23/eng/20230714
LC record available at https://lccn.loc.gov/2023028228
LC ebook record available at https://lccn.loc.gov/2023028229

Copyright © 2024 Bearport Publishing Company. All rights reserved. No part of this publication may be reproduced in whole or in part, stored in any retrieval system, or transmitted in any form or by any means, electronic, mechanical, photocopying, recording, or otherwise, without written permission from the publisher.

For more information, write to Bearport Publishing, 5357 Penn Avenue South, Minneapolis, MN 55419.

Contents

I Want to Lead 4

Be a Leader Now 22

Glossary 23

Index 24

Read More 24

Learn More Online. 24

About the Author 24

I Want to Lead

I live in a big city.

It has many people.

The mayor is our leader.

I want to be mayor someday!

The mayor works for everyone in the city.

The people who live there pick the mayor.

They **vote** for who they think will help the **community**.

There are many things mayors do.

Mayors help plan how to spend the city's money.

This money can pay for new roads or parks.

Mayors do not work alone.

They get help from the **city council**.

They all meet in a building called city hall.

The mayor and city council make rules for the city.

The rules are there to keep everybody safe.

Mayors learn ways to make the city better.

They listen to people who live there.

They also visit **businesses** in their city.

Sometimes, mayors talk to the people who fix the streets.

They may listen to the people who drive the city buses, too.

These people know what the city needs.

Mayors try to make their cities special.

They **celebrate** with the community at fun events.

They want other people to visit their city.

Being a mayor is a lot of work.

Taking care of a city is a big job.

But I think I could do it!

Be a Leader Now

There are many ways you can be a leader before you become mayor.

Treat others with kindness. Play with *everyone* at recess.

Send a letter or an email to your mayor about what your city needs.

Do what you can to help others. Give away clothes that do not fit anymore.

Glossary

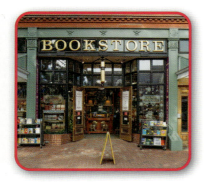

businesses places that sell things or provide services

celebrate to come together and enjoy a special event

city council a group of people who make rules for the city

community the people and places in an area where people live

vote to make a choice about someone or something

Index

businesses 14
city council 10, 13
city hall 10
listen 14, 16
money 8
rules 13
vote 6

Read More

Gaston, Stephanie. *Mayor (The Job of a Civic Leader).* Coral Springs, FL: Seahorse Publishing, 2023.

Mahoney, Emily Jankowski. *What Does the Mayor Do All Day? (What Do They Do?).* New York: Gareth Stevens Publishing, 2021.

Learn More Online

1. Go to **www.factsurfer.com** or scan the QR code below.
2. Enter **"To Be Mayor"** into the search box.
3. Click on the cover of this book to see a list of websites.

About the Author

Jenny Boothroyd likes to tour different city hall buildings. The one in her city has a great view of Lake Superior.